NORTH CAROLINA TEST PREP

Practice Test Book

End-of-Grade Reading Comprehension

Grade 3

ISBN 978-1466315013

CONTENTS

Section 1
Reading Mini-Tests

INTRODUCTION TO THE READING MINI-TESTS
For Parents, Teachers, and Tutors

How Reading is Assessed by the State of North Carolina

All North Carolina students take the End-of-Grade (EOG) Reading Comprehension test each year. The test assesses reading skills by having students read passages and answer reading comprehension questions about the passages. On the EOG Reading Comprehension test, students read 6 to 10 passages and answer 58 multiple-choice questions.

About the Reading Mini-Tests

This section of the practice test book contains passages and question sets similar to those on the EOG Reading Comprehension tests. However, students can take mini-tests instead of taking a complete practice test. Each mini-test has one passage for students to read. Students then answer 8 multiple-choice questions about the passage.

This section of the book is an effective way for students to build up to taking the full-length test. Students can focus on one passage and a small set of questions at a time. This will build confidence and help students become familiar with answering test questions. Students will gradually develop the skills they need to complete the full-length practice test in Section 3 of this book.

Reading Skills

The EOG Reading Comprehension test given by the state of North Carolina tests a specific set of skills. The full answer key at the end of the book identifies what skill each question is testing.

There are also key reading skills that students will need to understand to master the EOG Reading Comprehension test. The answer key includes additional information on these key skills so you can help the student gain understanding.

Reading Comprehension

Mini-Test 1

Instructions

Read the passage. The passage is followed by questions.

Read each question carefully. Then select the best answer. Fill in the circle for the correct answer.

The Naughty Boy

Kevin was a very active young child. He was naughty and would often play tricks on his friends and relatives. His tricks got worse as he grew older. Over time, everyone began to know Kevin as a troublemaker. At first, he really enjoyed all of the attention. He almost felt famous for his tricks.

One day, he was at his friend Jason's house. They were playing hide and seek. Kevin told Jason to hide from the others in his basement. Jason opened the door and started down the steps. Kevin locked the basement door behind him. Kevin put the key into his pocket and skipped away.

After a while, Jason became very scared. It was dark in the basement. As Jason began to cry, all his other friends tried to open the door. Jason's friend Max pushed on the door as hard as he could. But the door would not budge.

Eventually, Jason's mother heard the noise. She came downstairs to see what all the fuss was about. She unlocked the door with a spare key and hugged her son as he ran out. She then gathered the children together.

"Who did this?" she asked.

Kevin put his hand in the air.

"Me," he said, as he smiled.

Jason's mother sighed.

"You seem very proud, Kevin," she said. "But what you don't realize is that being well known for something isn't always a good thing. Sure, you might be known by all of your teachers and schoolmates, but it is for the wrong reason. Think how much better it would be if you were thought of as nice or hardworking."

Kevin's shoulders slumped.

"I guess so," he whispered.

1   Read these sentences from the passage.

Jason's friend Max pushed on the door as hard as he could. But the door would not budge.

What does the word *budge* mean in the sentence?

Ⓐ   Break

Ⓑ   Bend

Ⓒ   Move

Ⓓ   Listen

2   Which two words from the passage have about the **same** meaning?

Ⓐ   *friends, relatives*

Ⓑ   *naughty, tricks*

Ⓒ   *proud, nice*

Ⓓ   *famous, well-known*

3   Who is the main character in the passage?

Ⓐ   Kevin

Ⓑ   Jason's mother

Ⓒ   Jason

Ⓓ   Max

4   Read this sentence from the passage.

Kevin put the key into his pocket and skipped away.

What does the word *skipped* suggest about Kevin?

Ⓐ   He moved slowly.

Ⓑ   He was happy.

Ⓒ   He moved quietly.

Ⓓ   He was angry.

5   Which word **best** describes the trick that Kevin plays on Jason?

Ⓐ   Funny

Ⓑ   Mean

Ⓒ   Strange

Ⓓ   Silly

6 What is the second paragraph **mostly** about?

   Ⓐ   Why Kevin plays tricks

   Ⓑ   How children should not play in basements

   Ⓒ   A trick that Kevin plays on a friend

   Ⓓ   How a boy learns why he shouldn't play tricks

7 What happens **right after** Jason's mother comes downstairs?

   Ⓐ   She asks who locked Jason in the basement.

   Ⓑ   She lets Jason out of the basement.

   Ⓒ   She explains to Kevin why he should not play tricks.

   Ⓓ   She hears a noise coming from the basement.

8 How does Jason feel when he is locked in the basement?

   Ⓐ   Calm

   Ⓑ   Bored

   Ⓒ   Angry

   Ⓓ   Frightened

Reading Comprehension

Mini-Test 2

Instructions

Read the passage. The passage is followed by questions.

Read each question carefully. Then select the best answer. Fill in the circle for the correct answer.

Roger Federer

Roger Federer is a famous tennis player. He was born in Switzerland in 1981. Some people believe that he is the best tennis player ever. He became the world number one in 2005. He kept this rank for 237 weeks in a row. That is a record! He won 16 Grand Slam titles. That is also a record!

Roger plays well on clay, grass, and hard courts. However, he plays best on grass courts.

Wimbledon is a tennis contest held in Great Britain. Roger has won it six times. In 2008, he tried to win it for the sixth time in a row. He made the final. He was defeated by Spanish player Rafael Nadal. It was a close match. It was tough on both players. It was also great to watch. Some people say that it was the best tennis match ever played. This match also started a long row between the two players.

In 2009, Nadal was having knee problems. He was not well enough to compete in Wimbledon. Federer won that year. In 2010, Nadal beat Roger in the Wimbledon final. The two have competed in eight Grand Slam finals together. Nadal has won six of these.

In 2010, Roger lost his number one ranking. Nadal became world number one. At the start of 2011, Roger was ranked third in the world. He may come back and become number one again. To do this, he will need to beat Nadal.

1   Read this sentence from the passage.

This match also started a long row between the two players.

Which word means about the **same** as *row*?

Ⓐ   Game

Ⓑ   Chat

Ⓒ   Fight

Ⓓ   Problem

2   In paragraph 3, what does the word *defeated* mean?

Ⓐ   Beaten

Ⓑ   Watched

Ⓒ   Surprised

Ⓓ   Hurt

3   Where was Roger Federer born?

Ⓐ   Great Britain

Ⓑ   Switzerland

Ⓒ   Spain

Ⓓ   United States

4   What is the first paragraph **mainly** about?

    Ⓐ   Roger Federer's success

    Ⓑ   Roger Federer's family

    Ⓒ   Roger Federer's problems

    Ⓓ   Roger Federer's childhood

5   From the information in the passage, the reader can tell that Rafael Nadal –

    Ⓐ   dislikes playing Roger Federer

    Ⓑ   became a better player than Roger Federer

    Ⓒ   looked up to Roger Federer when he was young

    Ⓓ   plays better on clay than Roger Federer

6   Which detail from the passage is a **fact**?

    Ⓐ   Roger Federer is the best tennis player ever.

    Ⓑ   Roger Federer will become number one again.

    Ⓒ   Roger Federer was number one for 237 weeks in a row.

    Ⓓ   Roger Federer is a great player to watch.

7   Why didn't Nadal compete in Wimbledon in 2009?

   Ⓐ   He was too young.

   Ⓑ   He had knee problems.

   Ⓒ   He wasn't good enough.

   Ⓓ   He had won too many times.

8   How did Roger Federer **most likely** feel when he lost the 2008 Wimbledon final?

   Ⓐ   Calm

   Ⓑ   Upset

   Ⓒ   Proud

   Ⓓ   Scared

Reading Comprehension

Mini-Test 3

Instructions

Read the passage. The passage is followed by questions.

Read each question carefully. Then select the best answer. Fill in the circle for the correct answer.

A Bold Decision

Steven loved playing for his basketball team. Last year, they had won the state finals. This year, they were finding things much harder. There were only three games left in the season. Steven's team needed to win them all if they were going to the state playoffs. Near the end of the game, they were behind by six points. Steven had also hurt his knee when he fell on the court.

"Are you okay to play?" asked his coach.

Steven frowned at the pain in his knee.

"I'll be fine," he said.

Steven knew the risks of his decision. He could risk hurting his knee even more. Or he could choose not to play. He knew that not playing might cause his team to lose. As he rested before the final quarter, he decided to play through the pain. He felt that he was going to win this game for the team he loved.

As the quarter started, he caught the ball after the other team made a mistake. He bounced the ball down the court and threw the ball into the hoop. Steven smiled towards his coach on the sidelines. They were only four points behind now.

Steven kept playing well during the final quarter. He even scored a three point shot from the center of the court. With just two minutes left on the clock, Steven's team was only one point behind. Steven was passed the ball by his teammate. He ignored the pain in his knee and sprinted forward. He headed towards the end of the court. His feet left the ground. He sent his shot into the basket and earned his side two points. The final whistle blew seconds after. Steven's bold decision had won his team the game.

1   Read this sentence from the passage.

> **He even scored a three point shot from the center of the court.**

Which word could **best** be used in place of *center*?

Ⓐ   Edge

Ⓑ   Middle

Ⓒ   Back

Ⓓ   Front

2   Which two words from the passage have about the **same** meaning?

Ⓐ   *finals, games*

Ⓑ   *rested, play*

Ⓒ   *decision, choice*

Ⓓ   *bounced, threw*

3   What is Steven's bold decision?

Ⓐ   Deciding to play when he is hurt

Ⓑ   Deciding to take the final shot

Ⓒ   Deciding to win the game

Ⓓ   Deciding to try to make a three point shot

4   Read this sentence from the passage.

He ignored the pain in his knee and sprinted forward.

The word *sprinted* shows that Steven moved –

Ⓐ   quickly

Ⓑ   shakily

Ⓒ   quietly

Ⓓ   slowly

5   Why does Steven decide to play?

Ⓐ   He really wants his team to win.

Ⓑ   He does not want to upset his coach.

Ⓒ   He does not realize that he is hurt.

Ⓓ   He wants everyone to cheer for him.

6   What is the last paragraph **mainly** about?

Ⓐ   How Steven's team won the game

Ⓑ   How Steven felt at the end of the game

Ⓒ   Why the game was important to Steven

Ⓓ   How to shoot a basket correctly

7   Who is telling the story?

Ⓐ   Steven

Ⓑ   The coach

Ⓒ   Steven's teammate

Ⓓ   Someone not in the story

8   The author would probably describe Steven as –

Ⓐ   kind

Ⓑ   clever

Ⓒ   silly

Ⓓ   brave

Reading Comprehension

Mini-Test 4

Instructions

Read the passage. The passage is followed by questions.

Read each question carefully. Then select the best answer. Fill in the circle for the correct answer.

Rice Crispy Cakes

Rice crispy cakes are popular treats for children. They are easy to make too. First you will need some crispy rice cereal, butter, and a block of milk chocolate. You will also require a small bowl, a medium saucepan, a large saucepan, a baking tray, and patty cake holders.

What to Do

1. Start by pouring the crispy rice cereal into the small bowl.

2. Add 3 to 4 tablespoons of butter. It is a good idea to soften the butter first. Mix everything together with your hands.

3. You should now be able to fill the patty cake holders. Put a clump of the rice cereal mixture into each holder.

4. Next, you need to melt your block of chocolate. Fill a medium saucepan with water. Chop up about 2 ounces of chocolate. Place it in a small saucepan. Place the small saucepan in the medium saucepan. This will allow the hot water to gradually melt the bar of chocolate. When your chocolate has turned to a thick liquid, it is ready to add to your crispy rice mixture.

5. Carefully pour a small amount of melted chocolate onto each ball of crispy rice. Make sure that each rice crispy cake is covered.

6. Arrange each crispy cake on the baking tray and place in the oven.

7. Bake them at 350 degrees for about 30 minutes.

8. When they're done baking, take them out of the oven.

1 Read this sentence from the passage.

> **This will allow the hot water to gradually melt the bar of chocolate.**

What does the word *gradually* **most likely** mean?

Ⓐ   Nicely

Ⓑ   Slowly

Ⓒ   Firmly

Ⓓ   Quickly

2 Read these sentences from the passage.

> **First you will need some crispy rice cereal, butter, and a block of milk chocolate. You will also require a small bowl, a medium saucepan, a large saucepan, a baking tray, and patty cake holders.**

What would the author be **best** to use to give this information more clearly?

Ⓐ   Map

Ⓑ   List

Ⓒ   Diagram

Ⓓ   Timeline

3 What is probably the main purpose of softening the butter?

Ⓐ To make it easier to mix with the cereal

Ⓑ To help the chocolate melt

Ⓒ To make the crispy cake cook quicker

Ⓓ To make it easier to measure out

4 What is the **main** purpose of the passage?

Ⓐ To teach readers how to do something

Ⓑ To entertain readers with a story

Ⓒ To inform readers about crispy rice cereal

Ⓓ To compare different types of sweets

5 In Step 3, what does the word *clump* show?

Ⓐ Only a small amount of mixture should be used.

Ⓑ The mixture does not have to be a perfect shape.

Ⓒ The mixture is made of rice crispy cereal.

Ⓓ The mixture should be a smooth round ball.

6   In which step are the patty cake holders **first** needed?

(A)   Step 1

(B)   Step 2

(C)   Step 3

(D)   Step 4

7   Which of these would **most** help the reader make the rice crispy cakes?

(A)   A picture of a box of cereal

(B)   A list of different types of cereals

(C)   A photograph of a rice crispy cake

(D)   A timeline of the events

8   Which step does the photograph **most** help the reader complete?

(A)   Step 3

(B)   Step 4

(C)   Step 5

(D)   Step 6

Reading Comprehension

Mini-Test 5

Instructions

Read the passage. The passage is followed by questions.

Read each question carefully. Then select the best answer. Fill in the circle for the correct answer.

Sarah and Janet

Sarah and her sister Janet were always competing with each other. Sarah always wanted to outdo Janet. Janet always wanted to outdo Sarah.

They liked the same clothes, music, toys. They both wanted to be the fastest runner and the best volleyball player. They would even compete over who was the smartest. It drove their mother crazy.

"Why can't you girls just get along?" she would ask them time and time again.

They would just shrug and keep on trying to show off. One day, their mother had an idea to help them get along. She planned to take them shopping at the local mall. The girls were excited about taking a shopping trip.

When they arrived at the mall, they entered a clothing shop. Soon enough, the girls began fighting over the clothing.

"I want this dress," Sarah stated.

"No, I want that dress," Janet said.

"I'm having it because it will look better on me," Sarah said.

"It will not! It will look better on me," Janet said.

"Alright," said their mother quietly. "You can both have one."

The girls looked at each other. They were both confused. Usually their mother would buy them different clothes. She had never bought them the same thing before. The shopping trip continued. The girls bought a range of new identical clothes. They returned home unsure as to what was happening.

It all became clear the following day. The girls dressed for school in their own rooms and headed downstairs for breakfast. They were shocked to see that they were both wearing the same outfit. They began to argue about who should go and change their clothes.

"Nobody is going to change their clothes," said their mother. "You made these choices. You chose these clothes. Now you can see what your silly arguments have led to."

The girls giggled as they realized what their mother was saying.

1 Read this sentence from the passage.

They would even compete over who was the smartest.

What does the word *smartest* mean?

Ⓐ   The most smart

Ⓑ   Less smart

Ⓒ   One who is smart

Ⓓ   More smart

2 Read this sentence from the passage.

It all became clear the following day.

Which meaning of the word *clear* is used in the sentence?

Ⓐ   Able to be seen through

Ⓑ   Fine or nice

Ⓒ   Understood or known

Ⓓ   Sounding pleasant

3   What is the mother's **main** problem in the passage?

    Ⓐ   Her daughters have too many things.

    Ⓑ   Her daughters need more clothes.

    Ⓒ   Her daughters wear the same outfits.

    Ⓓ   Her daughters are always fighting.

4   Read this sentence from the passage.

"Why can't you girls just get along?" she would ask them time and time again.

What does the phrase "time and time again" suggest?

    Ⓐ   That the mother has asked the question for the last time

    Ⓑ   That the mother asks at the same time each day

    Ⓒ   That the mother has asked the question many times

    Ⓓ   That the mother asked the question once an hour

5   Where would this passage **most likely** be found?

    Ⓐ   In a book of poems

    Ⓑ   In a magazine

    Ⓒ   In a science textbook

    Ⓓ   In a book of short stories

6   What **most likely** happens next in the passage?

    Ⓐ   The girls go shopping again

    Ⓑ   The girls go to school looking the same

    Ⓒ   The girls put on a different matching outfit

    Ⓓ   The girls ask their father for help

7   What happens **right after** the girls come downstairs for breakfast?

    Ⓐ   They see that they are wearing the same thing.

    Ⓑ   They begin to argue.

    Ⓒ   They start giggling.

    Ⓓ   They get dressed for school.

8   If the passage was given another title, which title would **best** fit?

    Ⓐ   Being Your Best

    Ⓑ   How to Shop Well

    Ⓒ   Fighting Over Nothing

    Ⓓ   The Magic Dress

Reading Comprehension

Mini-Test 6

Instructions

Read the passage. The passage is followed by questions.

Read each question carefully. Then select the best answer. Fill in the circle for the correct answer.

No Time to Talk

May 23, 2011

Dear Principal Becker,

I understand that school is meant for learning. It is important to have good reading skills and to be able to solve math problems. But I think school is also important for another reason. It helps people learn to get along with others.

It may seem like lunchtime is not important. After all, I spend most lunchtimes just chatting to my friends. But this activity is more important than it looks.

I am learning how to get along with others. I am learning how to solve problems. I am finding out new things from people, and realizing my mistakes. I am learning how to stand up for myself. I am learning how to say sorry. These are all important skills to learn.

My problem is that the time for lunch and our other breaks keep getting shorter. I know this is happening so we can spend more time in class learning. But please do not forget that we are also learning in our lunchtimes. We are learning people skills. It is important that we have enough time to spend with our friends.

I ask that you consider making our lunch break longer. A little more time spent with friends each day would benefit everybody.

Best,

Simone Anderson

1   Read this sentence from the letter.

My problem is that the time for lunch and our other breaks keep getting shorter.

What does the word *shorter* mean?

Ⓐ   Less short

Ⓑ   The most short

Ⓒ   More short

Ⓓ   The least short

2   What does the word *benefit* mean in the last paragraph of the letter?

Ⓐ   Change

Ⓑ   Help

Ⓒ   Interest

Ⓓ   Harm

3   According to the letter, what does Simone learn at lunchtime?

Ⓐ   Math skills

Ⓑ   Reading skills

Ⓒ   People skills

Ⓓ   Drawing skills

4   Why did Simone write the letter?

Ⓐ   To persuade the principal to do something

Ⓑ   To entertain the principal

Ⓒ   To show the principal her writing skills

Ⓓ   To teach the principal how to do something

5   Which sentence **best** shows the main idea of the letter?

Ⓐ   *I understand that school is meant for learning.*

Ⓑ   *It may seem like lunchtime is not important.*

Ⓒ   *After all, I spend most lunchtimes just chatting to my friends.*

Ⓓ   *It is important that we have enough time to spend with our friends.*

6   What is the third paragraph **mostly** about?

Ⓐ   What Simone learns at lunchtime

Ⓑ   How long lunchtime lasts for

Ⓒ   What skills students should be taught

Ⓓ   What problems Simone has each day

7   Look at the web below.

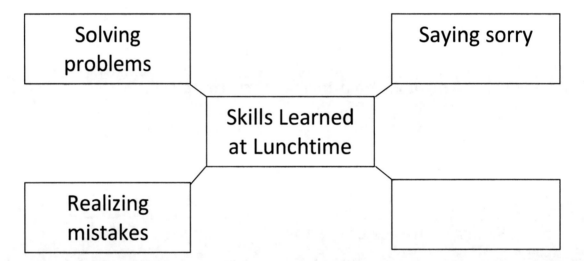

Which of these **best** completes the web?

Ⓐ   Solving math problems

Ⓑ   Standing up for yourself

Ⓒ   Managing time

Ⓓ   Reading well

8   Which statement is **most likely** true about Simone?

  Ⓐ   She writes a lot of letters to the principal.

  Ⓑ   She spends a lot of time in class talking.

  Ⓒ   She enjoys spending time with her friends.

  Ⓓ   She wishes that her friends were nicer.

Section 2
Vocabulary Quizzes

INTRODUCTION TO THE VOCABULARY QUIZZES
For Parents, Teachers, and Tutors

How Vocabulary is Assessed by the State of North Carolina

The EOG Reading Comprehension test includes multiple-choice questions that assess vocabulary skills. These questions follow each passage and are mixed in with the reading comprehension questions.

These questions require students to complete the following tasks:
- identify word meanings
- analyze word meanings in context
- understand and use suffixes
- understand and use prefixes
- identify antonyms (words that have opposite meanings)
- identify synonyms (words that have the same meaning)

About the Vocabulary Quizzes

This section of the practice test book contains six quizzes. Each quiz tests one vocabulary skill that is covered on the state test.

This section of the book covers all of the vocabulary skills assessed on the EOG Reading Comprehension test. The aim of the quizzes is to help ensure that students have all the vocabulary skills that they will need for the EOG Reading Comprehension test.

If students can master this section of the book, they will be ready to answer the vocabulary questions.

Quiz 1: Identify Word Meanings

1   What does the word *sparkled* mean in the sentence below?

   The bright dress sparkled in the sunlight.

   Ⓐ   Shifted

   Ⓑ   Shone

   Ⓒ   Waved

   Ⓓ   Rested

2   What does the word *boast* mean in the sentence below?

   Candy does boast about her good grades too much.

   Ⓐ   To chat

   Ⓑ   To brag

   Ⓒ   To study

   Ⓓ   To complain

3   What does the word *cart* mean in the sentence below?

   James had to cart all the books to the library.

   Ⓐ   A vehicle used to move goods

   Ⓑ   A table with wheels

   Ⓒ   To remove

   Ⓓ   To move or carry

Quiz 1: Identify Word Meanings

4 What does the word *adventure* suggest?

The game we played was quite an adventure.

Ⓐ The game was easy.

Ⓑ The game lasted a long time.

Ⓒ The game was exciting.

Ⓓ The game was played by many people.

5 What does the word *astonish* mean in the sentence below?

We wanted to astonish the class with our special project.

Ⓐ Amuse

Ⓑ Scare

Ⓒ Confuse

Ⓓ Amaze

6 What does the word *chuckle* mean in the sentence below?

My friends and I started to chuckle during the movie.

Ⓐ Cry

Ⓑ Laugh

Ⓒ Choke

Ⓓ Leave

Quiz 2: Analyze Word Meanings

1 If a chat between two people becomes *heated*, the people are –

Ⓐ getting angry

Ⓑ making each other laugh

Ⓒ feeling calm

Ⓓ speaking quietly

2 In which sentence does *skipped* mean the **same** as below?

Jan was busy, so she skipped breakfast.

Ⓐ Laura's sister skipped along the path.

Ⓑ Martin disliked the first song, so he skipped it.

Ⓒ Kevin hopped, skipped, and then jumped.

Ⓓ Anne skipped over the jump rope.

3 What does the word *wear* mean in the sentence?

The carpet was old and was starting to wear.

Ⓐ To tire someone out

Ⓑ To have clothing on

Ⓒ To damage something by rubbing

Ⓓ To pass time slowly

Quiz 2: Analyze Word Meanings

4 How is *slamming* a door different from *closing* a door?

   Ⓐ   The door is closed and locked.

   Ⓑ   The door is closed hard.

   Ⓒ   The door is closed quietly.

   Ⓓ   The door is closed and then opened.

5 Which word can be used to complete **both** sentences?

The weather was sunny and _____.
Jarred was asked to _____ the table.

   Ⓐ   clear

   Ⓑ   move

   Ⓒ   wipe

   Ⓓ   nice

6 What does the word *present* mean in the sentence?

Mr. Johnson opened his birthday present.

   Ⓐ   A gift

   Ⓑ   To give something

   Ⓒ   Taking place now

   Ⓓ   To happen

Quiz 3: Use Synonyms

1 Read the sentence below.

"I don't feel like going to school," Yani whined.

Which word is **closest** in meaning to *whined*?

Ⓐ Complained

Ⓑ Yelled

Ⓒ Whispered

Ⓓ Argued

2 Which word means about the **same** as *rush*?

Ⓐ Wander

Ⓑ Walk

Ⓒ Push

Ⓓ Hurry

3 Which two words have about the **same** meaning?

Ⓐ Spend, save

Ⓑ Strong, large

Ⓒ Tired, sleepy

Ⓓ Sharp, cut

Quiz 3: Use Synonyms

4   Read the sentence below.

At the end of the sad book, Alison started to weep.

Which word means about the **same** as *weep*?

Ⓐ   Read

Ⓑ   Laugh

Ⓒ   Cry

Ⓓ   Shout

5   Which word means about the **same** as *perhaps*?

Ⓐ   Always

Ⓑ   Maybe

Ⓒ   Certainly

Ⓓ   Later

6   Which two words have about the **same** meaning?

Ⓐ   Polite, rude

Ⓑ   Last, first

Ⓒ   Closed, shut

Ⓓ   Shiny, new

Quiz 4: Use Antonyms

1 Read the sentence below.

The visitor was due to arrive at noon.

Which word means the **opposite** of *arrive*?

Ⓐ Leave

Ⓑ Enter

Ⓒ Appear

Ⓓ Welcome

2 Which word means the **opposite** of *smooth*?

Ⓐ Fine

Ⓑ Rough

Ⓒ Silky

Ⓓ Level

3 Which two words have **opposite** meanings?

Ⓐ Brave, tough

Ⓑ Cook, burn

Ⓒ Correct, wrong

Ⓓ Football, baseball

Quiz 4: Use Antonyms

4   Read the sentence below.

The stamp was too common to be worth anything.

Which word means the **opposite** of *common*?

Ⓐ   Usual

Ⓑ   Dirty

Ⓒ   Clean

Ⓓ   Rare

5   Which word means the **opposite** of *outside*?

Ⓐ   Garden

Ⓑ   Indoors

Ⓒ   Beyond

Ⓓ   Past

6   Which two words have **opposite** meanings?

Ⓐ   Whisper, sound

Ⓑ   Present, gift

Ⓒ   Pop, snap

Ⓓ   Loud, quiet

Quiz 5: Use Prefixes

1 What does the word *resell* mean?

Ⓐ Sell more

Ⓑ Not sell

Ⓒ Sell before

Ⓓ Sell again

2 Which prefix can be added to the word *understand* to make a word meaning "not understand"?

Ⓐ pre-

Ⓑ re-

Ⓒ mis-

Ⓓ dis-

3 Which prefix should be added to the word to make the sentence correct?

Greg __zipped his coat and took it off.

Ⓐ un-

Ⓑ dis-

Ⓒ in-

Ⓓ mis-

Quiz 5: Use Prefixes

4   What does the word *dislike* mean?

Ⓐ   Like more

Ⓑ   Not like

Ⓒ   Like before

Ⓓ   Like again

5   Which prefix can be added to the word *kind* to make a word meaning "not kind"?

Ⓐ   un-

Ⓑ   in-

Ⓒ   mis-

Ⓓ   dis-

6   Which word means "pay again"?

Ⓐ   Prepay

Ⓑ   Repay

Ⓒ   Mispay

Ⓓ   Unpay

Quiz 6: Use Suffixes

1   What does the word *loudest* mean?

    Ⓐ   Someone who is loud

    Ⓑ   More loud

    Ⓒ   The most loud

    Ⓓ   In a way that is loud

2   Which suffix can be added to the word *fear* to make a word meaning "without fear"?

    Ⓐ   -less

    Ⓑ   -ful

    Ⓒ   -ing

    Ⓓ   -ed

3   Which suffix should be added to the word to make the sentence correct?

    Corey neat__ folded his clothes.

    Ⓐ   -ful

    Ⓑ   -est

    Ⓒ   -er

    Ⓓ   -ly

Quiz 6: Use Suffixes

4   What does the word *cheerful* mean?

   Ⓐ   Having cheer

   Ⓑ   The most cheer

   Ⓒ   Someone who has cheer

   Ⓓ   Less cheer

5   Which suffix can be added to the word *garden* to make a word meaning "one who gardens"?

   Ⓐ   -er

   Ⓑ   -ing

   Ⓒ   -s

   Ⓓ   -ed

6   In which word is the suffix *–ing* used?

   Ⓐ   String

   Ⓑ   Acting

   Ⓒ   Anything

   Ⓓ   Swing

Section 3
End-of-Grade
Reading Comprehension
Practice Test

INTRODUCTION TO THE READING PRACTICE TEST
For Parents, Teachers, and Tutors

How Reading is Assessed by the State of North Carolina

All North Carolina students take the End-of-Grade (EOG) Reading Comprehension test each year. The test assesses reading skills by having students read passages and answer reading comprehension questions about the passages. On the EOG Reading Comprehension test, students read 6 to 10 passages and answer 58 multiple-choice questions.

About the EOG Reading Comprehension Practice Test

This section of the book contains a practice test just like the real EOG Reading Comprehension test. It has 8 passages and a total of 58 multiple-choice questions. The questions cover all the skills tested on the EOG Reading Comprehension test, and have the same formats. In short, taking this practice test is just like taking the real EOG Reading Comprehension test.

Students are expected to complete the real EOG Reading Comprehension test in 140 minutes, but are allowed up to 240 minutes. You can use the same time limit, or you can choose not to time the test. If you time the test, it is recommended that the student be given a 3 minute break each hour.

Students complete the EOG Reading Comprehension test by marking their answers on an answer sheet. An optional answer sheet is included in the back of the book.

Reading Skills

The EOG Reading Comprehension test assesses a specific set of skills. The full answer key at the end of the book identifies what skill each question is testing. There are also key reading skills that students will need to understand to master the test. The answer key includes additional information on these key skills so you can help the student gain understanding.

End-of-Grade

Reading Comprehension

Practice Test

Instructions

Read the passages. Each passage is followed by questions.

Read each question carefully. Then select the best answer. Fill in the circle for the correct answer.

Yard Sales

A yard sale is when you sell items in your front yard. People often have yard sales to get rid of unwanted items. It can also be a good way to make some extra money. Here are some good tips on how to have a good yard sale.

Finding the Items

1. You need a lot of items to sell. Search your home for all your unwanted items. Make sure everyone in the family joins in. Try to get a large range of items.

2. Clean out the garage or basement. Many people have a store of old stuff somewhere. Offer to clean up this area. As you do, collect everything you think you can sell.

3. Ask other people you know to join in. Many people have junk lying around they want to get rid of. They may be happy to give it to you to sell.

Setting It Up

1. Collect everything you have to sell. It is a good idea to make everything look neat and tidy. If you have clothes, wash them and hang them up. Dust old items so they look their best.

2. People will need to know how much each item is. Put a sticker on each item and write the price on it.

3. Set up tables in your front yard to place all the items on. If you are placing items on the ground, put them on a sheet or blanket.

4. Collect some change. People will often pay in notes. Make sure you have plenty of coins to give as change.

Getting a Crowd

1. You want lots of people to come to your yard sale. Here are some things you should do:
   - Tell all your friends
   - Put notices on notice boards
   - Put up flyers
   - Put an ad in the local newspaper
   - Put a sign at the end of your street

2. Make it easy for people to find the yard sale. Put balloons at the end of your street and in your front yard.

Time to Sell

1. Now it is time to sell your items. Remember that you are selling things you don't really want. Don't try to sell your items for too much. If people suggest a lower price, take it!

2. If items are not selling, lower the prices. It is better to sell items for something than to have to pack them all up again.

Popular Yard Sale Items
children's toys
clothes
building materials
furniture
kitchen items
books and movies

1   Read this sentence from the passage.

People often have yard sales to get rid of unwanted items.

What does the word *unwanted* mean?

Ⓐ   Less wanted

Ⓑ   Used to be wanted

Ⓒ   More wanted

Ⓓ   Not wanted

2   Why should you put balloons in your front yard?

Ⓐ   So people feel good about buying

Ⓑ   So you can sell them

Ⓒ   So people can find your yard sale

Ⓓ   So you can put prices on them

3   If the passage was given another title, which of the following would **best** fit?

Ⓐ   How to Make Money

Ⓑ   How to Hold a Yard Sale

Ⓒ   The Amazing Yard Sale

Ⓓ   Cleaning Up Your House

4   Read this sentence from the passage.

It is a good idea to make everything look neat and tidy.

Which word means the **opposite** of *neat*?

Ⓐ   Messy

Ⓑ   Clean

Ⓒ   Dirty

Ⓓ   Nice

5   Which section of the passage describes how to let people know about your yard sale?

Ⓐ   Finding the Items

Ⓑ   Setting It Up

Ⓒ   Getting a Crowd

Ⓓ   Time to Sell

6   According to the passage, which of the following should you do **first**?

Ⓐ   Put up flyers

Ⓑ   Clean all the items

Ⓒ   Put stickers on the items

Ⓓ   Lower the prices

7   How does the information in the table help the reader?

    Ⓐ   It explains how much money can be made.

    Ⓑ   It shows what sort of items to collect.

    Ⓒ   It shows how to price items.

    Ⓓ   It explains why you should have a yard sale.

The Wiggly Worm

The worm is one of nature's
most wonderful of creatures,
as it slinks beneath the soil,
with all its special features.

The worm is an explorer,
of both soft and well-worn land,
on a journey through the landscape,
unearthing stones, loose earth, and sand.

Though they barely see above the grass,
they see all beneath the ground,
hiding amongst the flower beds,
as they wiggle round and round.

Their bodies are long and slender
and as light as summer's breeze,
gilding shapes beneath the surface,
with slow and steady ease.

They're the envy of the rhino,
the hippopotamus, and ape,
and all the other animals that lack
one single beautiful shape.

So when you see the wiggly worm,
smile at his simple form,
and ponder his adventures,
in the earth all wet and warm.

8   Read this line from the poem.

they see all beneath the ground,

Which word means the **opposite** of *beneath*?

Ⓐ   Below

Ⓑ   Above

Ⓒ   Far

Ⓓ   Along

9   The poet would **most likely** describe worms as –

Ⓐ   scary

Ⓑ   amazing

Ⓒ   dirty

Ⓓ   boring

10   What is the rhyme pattern of each stanza of the poem?

   Ⓐ   The second and fourth lines rhyme.

   Ⓑ   There are two pairs of rhyming lines.

   Ⓒ   The first and last lines rhyme.

   Ⓓ   None of the lines rhyme.

11   Which line from the poem contains a **simile**?

   Ⓐ   *as it slinks beneath the soil,*

   Ⓑ   *hiding amongst the flower beds,*

   Ⓒ   *and as light as summer's breeze,*

   Ⓓ   *So when you see the wiggly worm,*

12 Which words from the poem describe what a worm looks like?

Ⓐ   *soft and well-worn*

Ⓑ   *long and slender*

Ⓒ   *slow and steady*

Ⓓ   *wet and warm*

13 Read this line from the poem.

in the earth all wet and warm.

Which literary device does the author use in this line?

Ⓐ   Simile

Ⓑ   Metaphor

Ⓒ   Alliteration

Ⓓ   Personification

Robert De Niro

Robert De Niro is an American actor. He is known as one of the finest actors of his time. He has starred in a number of blockbuster films. He has also won many awards.

He was born in 1943 in New York City. De Niro left high school at the age of sixteen. He wanted to have a career in acting. He dreamed of appearing in Hollywood films. He studied acting between 1959 and 1963. He then took part in several small films.

His first major film role arrived in 1973. It was in the film *Bang the Drum Slowly*. After this, he won a role in the film *The Godfather Part II*. The film is one of the greatest films in history. He won the Academy Award for Best Supporting Actor for this role. It was the start of a great career. He was then given the lead role in many films.

During this time, he became good friends with Martin Scorsese. Scorsese was a successful director. They began to work together often. Their first film together was *Mean Streets* in 1973. De Niro won the Academy Award for Best Actor for this role. In 1980, he starred in the film *Raging Bull*. Scorsese was the director again. And again, De Niro won an Academy Award.

His career continued. Over three decades, he has starred in many films. These have even included comedies like *Meet the Parents* and *Analyze This*.

Robert De Niro Films

Year	Title
1973	*Bang the Drum Slowly*
1974	*The Godfather Part II*
1976	*Taxi Driver*
1977	*New York, New York*
1980	*Raging Bull*
1986	*The Mission*
1987	*The Untouchables*
1988	*Midnight Run*
1990	*Goodfellas*
1991	*Backdraft*
1991	*Cape Fear*
1993	*A Bronx Tale*
1995	*Casino*
1995	*Heat*
1998	*Ronin*
1999	*Analyze This*
2000	*Meet the Parents*
2002	*Showtime*
2006	*The Good Shepherd*
2009	*Everybody's Fine*
2011	*Limitless*

14 Read this sentence from the passage.

He is known as one of the finest actors of his time.

As it is used in the sentence, what does *finest* mean?

Ⓐ   Best

Ⓑ   Smallest

Ⓒ   Rarest

Ⓓ   Nicest

15 What does the table **best** show?

Ⓐ   How many awards De Niro has won

Ⓑ   How many times De Niro worked with Scorsese

Ⓒ   How long De Niro has been acting for

Ⓓ   How De Niro chose his roles

16   Which sentence from the passage is an **opinion**?

    Ⓐ   *Robert De Niro is an American actor.*

    Ⓑ   *He was born in 1943 in New York City.*

    Ⓒ   *The film is one of the greatest films in history.*

    Ⓓ   *He won the Academy Award for Best Supporting Actor for this role.*

17   How is the passage **mainly** organized?

    Ⓐ   A solution to a problem is described.

    Ⓑ   A question is asked and then answered.

    Ⓒ   A series of events are described in order.

    Ⓓ   Two different actors are compared.

18 According to the passage, how are Robert De Niro and Martin Scorsese **alike**?

Ⓐ   They were both born in New York.

Ⓑ   They are both good actors.

Ⓒ   They both direct movies.

Ⓓ   They are both successful.

19 The passage was probably written **mainly** to –

Ⓐ   encourage people to become actors

Ⓑ   describe the life of Robert De Niro

Ⓒ   tell a funny story about a movie star

Ⓓ   teach readers how to break into films

20 What type of passage is "Robert De Niro"?

Ⓐ Biography

Ⓑ Short story

Ⓒ Diary

Ⓓ News article

A Letter to My Favorite Author

July 1, 2011

Dear Simeon,

I am writing to tell you what a huge fan I am of your work. I have enjoyed your books since I was eight years old. I read a story in the newspaper that said you were ill. It made me feel sad. I wanted to write just to tell you how much I like your work. And that I hope you feel better soon too!

My love for your work began with your first book. *The Singing Swordfish* was so well-written. The pictures also helped to bring your words to life. I laughed so hard I cried the first time I read the book! From then on, I was hooked on your every word. I cannot imagine a better children's author existing anywhere else in the world. If there is one, I would certainly like to know about them too! If I had to choose which of your books was my favorite, it would be *The Shining Light of the Silver Sunshine*. That story was such an adventure from start to finish. Your book *Rainy Day* is also a favorite. It made me think a lot. And of course, I love *Just Lazing Around* as well. It always makes me laugh.

I hope that you feel better soon. You have given so much joy to so many people. Take care and thank you for all of the memories and moments of joy that you have given me.

Yours sincerely,

Kyle Harper

21 Read this sentence from the letter.

From then on, I was hooked on your every word.

What does the phrase "hooked on" mean?

Ⓐ   Very keen on

Ⓑ   Confused by

Ⓒ   Bent

Ⓓ   Owned

22 Read this sentence from the letter.

I cannot imagine a better children's author existing anywhere else in the world.

Which word means about the **same** as *existing*?

Ⓐ   Living

Ⓑ   Writing

Ⓒ   Working

Ⓓ   Thinking

23 According to the letter, why does Kyle decide to write to Simeon?

Ⓐ   He is asked to by his mother.

Ⓑ   He wants to be sent a free book.

Ⓒ   He wants her to write another book.

Ⓓ   He reads that she is ill.

24 According to the letter, which book did Kyle read **first**?

Ⓐ   *The Singing Swordfish*

Ⓑ   *The Shining Light of the Silver Sunshine*

Ⓒ   *Rainy Day*

Ⓓ   *Just Lazing Around*

25   The reader can tell that Kyle –

Ⓐ   no longer reads Simeon's books

Ⓑ   wants to be a writer someday

Ⓒ   has read many of Simeon's books

Ⓓ   started reading because he was ill

26   What is the first paragraph **mainly** about?

Ⓐ   Why Kyle is writing to Simeon

Ⓑ   When Kyle started reading Simeon's books

Ⓒ   Which book of Simeon's is Kyle's favorite

Ⓓ   How Kyle reads the newspaper

The New York Times

The New York Times is an American newspaper. It was founded in New York. It was first printed in 1851. The first issue cost just 1 cent to buy. It is printed each day. Each issue is read by around one million people. The newspaper has won 106 Pulitzer Prizes. A Pulitzer Prize is an award given for excellent reporting. This is more than any other newspaper or magazine.

The New York Times is the largest local newspaper in the United States. It is also the third largest newspaper overall. Only *The Wall Street Journal* and *USA Today* are read by more people.

Even though it is still popular, it sells fewer copies today than in the past. In 1990, it was read by over a million people. By 2010, it was being read by less than a million people. This change has occurred for most printed newspapers. The main reason is that people can read the news on the Internet for free.

The newspaper's motto is "All the News That's Fit to Print." This appears printed in the top corner of the front page.

The newspaper has many different sections. It covers news, business, and science. It also covers sport, home, and fashion. It has sections for travel, food, art, and movies. It is also known for its difficult crossword puzzles.

In 2011, each issue sold for $2. However, the Sunday issue is larger. It is sold for $5.

27 Read this sentence from the passage.

It was founded in New York.

What does the word *founded* mean in the sentence?

Ⓐ   Sold

Ⓑ   Discovered

Ⓒ   Started

Ⓓ   Lost

28 Read this sentence from the passage.

The newspaper's motto is "All the News That's Fit to Print."

As it is used in this sentence, what does *fit* mean?

Ⓐ   Ready

Ⓑ   Healthy

Ⓒ   Right

Ⓓ   Known

29 According to the passage, how is *The Wall Street Journal* **different** from *The New York Times*?

Ⓐ   It is read by more people.

Ⓑ   It has won more awards.

Ⓒ   It costs less to buy.

Ⓓ   It has fewer sections.

30 According to the passage, why are fewer copies of *The New York Times* sold today than in the past?

Ⓐ   It costs too much.

Ⓑ   People read the news online.

Ⓒ   People buy other newspapers instead.

Ⓓ   It has too many sections.

31   Which word **best** describes the tone of the passage?

Ⓐ   Funny

Ⓑ   Serious

Ⓒ   Lively

Ⓓ   Hopeful

32   Which detail **best** shows that *The New York Times* is successful?

Ⓐ   It is printed seven days a week.

Ⓑ   Its price has increased to $2.

Ⓒ   It has a motto.

Ⓓ   It has won 106 Pulitzer Prizes.

33   Look at the web below.

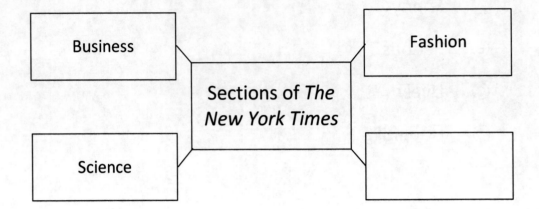

Which word **best** completes the web?

Ⓐ   Gardening

Ⓑ   Comics

Ⓒ   Music

Ⓓ   Travel

The Top of the Tower

Toby had a fear of heights. He had carried it with him since he was an infant. As a teenager, his fear had only become worse. He talked to his father about it one day.

"I have had enough Dad," he said. "I would love to go rock climbing with my friends. But every time I get too high, I feel sick."

His dad paused as he thought about his son's problem.

"Well Toby," he said quietly, "I can help you. But you will need to face your fear. Are you ready?"

Toby was quiet for a moment.

"I am ready!" he replied bravely.

Toby's father picked up the keys and walked toward the front door.

"We're going into the city!" his father said.

Toby knew what was coming. Toby lived in Paris, France. Located in the heart of Paris, was one of the world's tallest landmarks. It was the Eiffel Tower. Toby knew that visitors were allowed to climb to the very top. The view overlooked the entire city. Nothing was said between the pair as they drove into the city.

They had arrived at the Eiffel Tower when Toby looked up at it and gasped. His stomach turned over.

"I'm not sure if I can do this," he said nervously.

Toby's father sensed his son's worries.

"Don't worry," he said. "I will be with you every step of the way. This is the day that you beat your fears."

Toby stared up at the giant tower. He took a deep breath as they stepped through the entrance. As his father held his hand, they made their way, step by step, towards the top of the building. Once they reached the top, Toby stepped out from the shadows and onto the ledge.

"Wow, Dad!" he said excitedly as he looked over Paris.

"I told you there was nothing to worry about," came the reply.

34 Read this sentence from the passage.

> **Located in the heart of Paris, was one of the world's tallest landmarks.**

What does the phrase "heart of" mean in the sentence?

Ⓐ Streets of

Ⓑ Edge of

Ⓒ Center of

Ⓓ City of

35 Read this sentence from the passage.

> **Nothing was said between the pair as they drove into the city.**

Why was Toby **most likely** quiet?

Ⓐ He was fighting with his father.

Ⓑ He was feeling scared.

Ⓒ He was excited.

Ⓓ He was having a nap.

36   Where would this passage **most likely** be found?

    Ⓐ   In a book of poems

    Ⓑ   In a magazine

    Ⓒ   In a travel guide

    Ⓓ   In a book of short stories

37   Read this sentence from the passage.

> **As his father held his hand, they made their way, step by step, towards the top of the building.**

What do the words "step by step" suggest?

    Ⓐ   They moved quite slowly.

    Ⓑ   They walked a long way.

    Ⓒ   They raced each other.

    Ⓓ   They made a lot of noise.

38   Who is telling the story?

  Ⓐ   Toby

  Ⓑ   Toby's father

  Ⓒ   A friend of Toby's

  Ⓓ   Someone not in the story

39   The **main** theme of the passage is about –

  Ⓐ   taking chances

  Ⓑ   overcoming fears

  Ⓒ   making friends

  Ⓓ   asking for help

40 Which word **best** describes Toby?

Ⓐ Friendly

Ⓑ Funny

Ⓒ Brave

Ⓓ Shy

Visiting Day

July 5

Dear Connie,

Today is always one of my favorite days. It was a Tuesday, the day that I visit my grandmother. She lives in a nursing home where she can be taken care of. My grandmother has been unwell for a long time. She sometimes forgets some of the things she has done and the people she has met. I am sad to say that she sometimes forgets my mother and I. But I understand it is just because she is sick. Happily, today was one of the better days. She was smiling and seemed to know exactly where she was and who had come to visit. She even giggled as we told her what we had been doing over the last few weeks.

We talked for hours about when I was younger and I used to spend time at her place. We talked about the time that we went to the carnival and she held my hand on every ride. She even took me on every roller coaster! I was never scared when I was around my grandmother. I knew what a wonderful life she had lived. She was not afraid of anything and always kept me safe.

I always try to be positive when I visit my grandmother. It is easy on days like today when she is cheerful. However, I know next time she might be confused and very quiet. I always keep smiling though, because I remember her as the great grandmother she has always been. I only hope that we get more days like today where we can share the stories of our lives.

Love,
Ella

41   Read this sentence from the passage.

I always try to be positive when I visit my grandmother.

Which meaning of the word *positive* is used in the sentence?

Ⓐ   Certain or sure

Ⓑ   Upbeat and cheery

Ⓒ   Having good results

Ⓓ   A type of charge

42   Which two words from the passage have **opposite** meanings?

Ⓐ   *Unwell, ill*

Ⓑ   *Scared, afraid*

Ⓒ   *Wonderful, safe*

Ⓓ   *Cheerful, sad*

43   Which detail **best** shows that Ella's grandmother was happy?

Ⓐ   She smiled and giggled.

Ⓑ   She talked about the past.

Ⓒ   She held Ella's hand.

Ⓓ   She forgot where she was.

44 According to the passage, what is Ella's grandmother's **main** problem?

    Ⓐ   She cannot walk far.

    Ⓑ   She feels lonely.

    Ⓒ   She forgets things.

    Ⓓ   She sleeps too much.

45 Which word **best** describes Ella's feelings toward her grandmother?

    Ⓐ   Curious

    Ⓑ   Understanding

    Ⓒ   Amazed

    Ⓓ   Scared

46 What do Ella and her grandmother do together?

    Ⓐ   Go for a walk

    Ⓑ   Paint pictures

    Ⓒ   Watch a movie

    Ⓓ   Talk about the past

47   Based on the passage, how often does Ella **most likely** visit her grandmother?

Ⓐ   Every day

Ⓑ   Once a week

Ⓒ   Once a month

Ⓓ   Twice a year

48   What type of passage is "Visiting Day"?

Ⓐ   Short story

Ⓑ   Science fiction story

Ⓒ   Letter

Ⓓ   Fable

The West Moor Sports Camp

The health of our children is important. Good health means eating well and being active. Children should take part in sports or other activities often. This isn't always easy. In cities, it can be hard to find activities to do. Don't be alarmed, though. The West Moor Sports Camp can help!

The West Moor Sports Camp is an outdoor camp for people of all ages. Children can enjoy outdoor activities. They can also make new friends. All while the parents relax, knowing that their children are safe.

The West Moor Sports Camp is located among lush fields. There is a lot of open space for youngsters to run around and enjoy themselves. There are many games and sports that they can take part in. These include football, soccer, baseball, basketball, athletics, and tennis. There are also fitness classes that children can take part in. Parents can even join in if they wish to.

There are many benefits to the camp. The first is that children will take part in a fitness program that they will enjoy! They will become fitter while having fun! The second is that children will make new friends. They will learn how to work with other children. It may also help children develop good fitness habits.

Many children find that they enjoy playing sports. It becomes a new interest. In the age of computer games, this is a great thing!

So visit our website today to find out more. Give your children a better future!

49 Read this sentence from the passage.

In cities, it can be hard to find activities to do.

Which word means the **opposite** of *hard*?

Ⓐ Cheap

Ⓑ Difficult

Ⓒ Easy

Ⓓ Costly

50 In the first paragraph, what does the word *alarmed* mean?

Ⓐ Worried

Ⓑ Lazy

Ⓒ Confused

Ⓓ Silly

51 How is the first paragraph **mainly** organized?

   Ⓐ   A problem is described and then a solution is given.

   Ⓑ   Events are described in the order they occur.

   Ⓒ   Facts are given to support an argument.

   Ⓓ   A question is asked and then answered.

52 Read this sentence from the passage.

   The West Moor Sports Camp is located among lush fields.

What does the word *lush* suggest about the fields?

   Ⓐ   They are large.

   Ⓑ   They are shaded.

   Ⓒ   They are green.

   Ⓓ   They are busy.

53 According to the passage, which sport is offered at the camp?

Ⓐ Golf

Ⓑ Tennis

Ⓒ Swimming

Ⓓ Volleyball

54 The passage was probably written **mainly** to –

Ⓐ encourage parents to send their children to the camp

Ⓑ compare children today with children in the past

Ⓒ describe the history of a camp

Ⓓ inform readers about the benefits of exercise

55   Which sentence is included **mainly** to persuade the reader?

   Ⓐ   *The West Moor Sports Camp is an outdoor camp for people of all ages.*

   Ⓑ   *There are many games and sports that they can take part in.*

   Ⓒ   *Many children find that they enjoy playing sports.*

   Ⓓ   *Give your children a better future!*

56   The passage is **most** like –

   Ⓐ   an essay

   Ⓑ   an advertisement

   Ⓒ   a short story

   Ⓓ   a news article

57   Look at the diagram below.

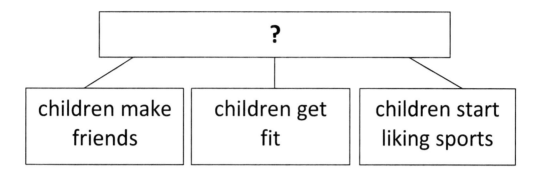

Which of these **best** fits in the empty box?

Ⓐ Problems that Children Have

Ⓑ Benefits of the Camp

Ⓒ Things to Do

Ⓓ City Kids

58   Which information would be **least** useful to a student trying to decide if they want to go to the camp?

Ⓐ *The West Moor Sports Camp is an outdoor camp for people of all ages.*

Ⓑ *The West Moor Sports Camp is located among lush fields.*

Ⓒ *There are many games and sports that they can take part in.*

Ⓓ *There are also fitness classes that children can take part in.*

END OF TEST

Answer Key

The End-of-Grade Reading Comprehension test given by the state of North Carolina assesses a specific set of skills. The answer key identifies what skill each question is testing.

The answer key also includes notes on key reading skills that students will need to understand to master the test. Use the notes to review the questions with students so they gain a full understanding of these key reading skills.

Section 1: Reading Mini-Tests

Mini-Test 1

The Naughty Boy

Question	Answer	Reading Skill
1	C	Use context to determine the meaning of words
2	D	Identify and use synonyms
3	A	Identify the main character
4	B	Understand and analyze word use
5	B	Draw conclusions based on information in a passage
6	C	Understand and analyze the plot of a passage
7	B	Identify the sequence of events
8	D	Draw conclusions about characters

Mini-Test 2

Roger Federer

Question	Answer	Reading Skill
1	C	Use context to determine the meaning of words
2	A	Use context to determine the meaning of words
3	B	Locate facts and details in a passage
4	A	Identify the main idea
5	B	Draw conclusions based on information in a passage
6	C	Distinguish between fact and opinion*
7	B	Understand cause and effect
8	B	Make inferences based on information in a passage

*Key Reading Skill: Fact and Opinion

A fact is a statement that can be proven to be correct. An opinion is a statement that cannot be proven to be correct. An opinion is what somebody thinks about something. The sentence given in answer choice C is a fact. The other sentences are opinions.

Mini-Test 3

A Bold Decision

Question	Answer	Reading Skill
1	B	Use context to determine the meaning of words
2	C	Identify and use synonyms
3	A	Understand and analyze the plot of a passage
4	A	Understand and analyze word use
5	A	Draw conclusions about characters
6	A	Identify the main idea
7	D	Identify point of view*
8	D	Make inferences about an author's opinion or viewpoint

*Key Reading Skill: Point of View

This question is asking about the point of view of the passage. There are three main points of view. They are:

- First person – the story is told by a narrator who is a character in the story. The use of the words *I*, *my*, or *we* indicate a first person point of view. *Example: I went for a hike in the mountains. After a while, my legs began to ache.*
- Second person – the story is told by referring to the reader as "you." *Example: You are hiking in the mountains. After a while, your legs begin to ache.*
- Third person – the story is told by a person outside the story. *Example: Jacky went for a hike in the mountains. After a while, her legs began to ache.*

The story has a third person point of view. It is told by someone who is not in the story.

Mini-Test 4

Rice Crispy Cakes

Question	Answer	Reading Skill
1	B	Use context to determine the meaning of words
2	B	Identify the purpose of text features
3	A	Make inferences based on information in a passage
4	A	Identify the author's main purpose
5	B	Understand and analyze word use
6	C	Understand written directions
7	C	Analyze the use of features such as maps, graphs, and photographs
8	B	Understand and analyze illustrations and photographs

Mini-Test 5

Sarah and Janet

Question	Answer	Reading Skill
1	A	Use prefixes and suffixes to determine the meaning of a word*
2	C	Use words with multiple meanings*
3	D	Identify the main problem in a passage
4	C	Understand and analyze word use
5	D	Identify different types of texts
6	B	Make predictions about characters
7	A	Identify the sequence of events
8	C	Identify the main idea*

*Key Reading Skill: Prefixes and Suffixes

A prefix is a word part that is placed at the start of a word, such as *un-* or *dis-*. A suffix is a word part that is placed at the end of a word, such as *-less* or *-ly.* The word *smartest* is the base word *smart* with the suffix *-est* added to the end. The meaning of *smartest* is "the most smart."

*Key Reading Skill: Multiple Meanings

Some words have more than one meaning. These words are known as homonyms. All the answer choices are possible meanings for the word *clear*. The correct answer is the one that states the meaning of the word *clear* as it is used in the sentence.

*Key Reading Skill: Main Idea

One way that identifying the main idea is tested is by asking what would be another good title for the passage. The correct answer is a title that describes what the passage is mainly about.

Mini-Test 6

No Time to Talk

Question	Answer	Reading Skill
1	C	Use prefixes and suffixes to determine the meaning of a word*
2	B	Use context to determine the meaning of words
3	C	Locate facts and details in a passage
4	A	Identify the author's main purpose
5	D	Identify the main idea
6	A	Identify the main idea
7	B	Summarize information given in a passage
8	C	Make inferences based on information in a passage

*Key Reading Skill: Prefixes and Suffixes

A prefix is a word part that is placed at the start of a word, such as *un-* or *dis-*. A suffix is a word part that is placed at the end of a word, such as *-less* or *-ly.* The word *shorter* is the base word *short* with the suffix *-er* added to the end. The meaning of *shorter* is "more short."

Section 2: Vocabulary Quizzes

Quiz 1: Identify Word Meanings

Question	Answer
1	B
2	B
3	D
4	C
5	D
6	B

Quiz 2: Analyze Word Meanings

Question	Answer
1	A
2	B
3	C
4	B
5	A
6	A

Quiz 3: Use Synonyms

Question	Answer
1	A
2	D
3	C
4	C
5	B
6	C

Quiz 4: Use Antonyms

Question	Answer
1	A
2	B
3	C
4	D
5	B
6	D

Quiz 5: Use Prefixes

Question	Answer
1	D
2	C
3	A
4	B
5	A
6	B

Quiz 6: Use Suffixes

Question	Answer
1	C
2	A
3	D
4	A
5	A
6	B

Section 3: End-of Grade Reading Comprehension Practice Test

Question	Answer	Reading Skill
1	D	Use prefixes and suffixes to determine the meaning of a word*
2	C	Draw conclusions based on information in a passage
3	B	Identify the main idea*
4	A	Identify and use antonyms
5	C	Use text features to locate information
6	B	Identify the sequence of events
7	B	Understand information in graphs, charts, or tables
8	B	Identify and use antonyms
9	B	Make inferences about an author's opinion or viewpoint
10	A	Identify the characteristics of poems
11	C	Understand and analyze literary techniques (simile)*
12	B	Identify the purpose of specific information
13	C	Understand and analyze literary techniques (alliteration)*
14	A	Use words with multiple meanings*
15	C	Understand information in graphs, charts, or tables
16	C	Distinguish between fact and opinion*
17	C	Identify how a passage is organized*
18	D	Compare and contrast based on information in a passage
19	B	Identify the author's main purpose
20	A	Identify different types of texts*
21	A	Identify the meaning of phrases
22	A	Identify and use synonyms
23	D	Understand cause and effect
24	A	Identify the sequence of events
25	C	Draw conclusions based on information in a passage
26	A	Identify the main idea
27	C	Use context to determine the meaning of words
28	C	Use words with multiple meanings*
29	A	Compare and contrast based on information in a passage
30	B	Understand cause and effect
31	B	Identify the tone of a passage*
32	D	Identify details that support a conclusion
33	D	Summarize information given in a passage
34	C	Identify the meaning of phrases
35	B	Make inferences about characters
36	D	Identify different types of texts
37	A	Understand and analyze word use
38	D	Identify point of view*

39	B	Identify and summarize the theme of a passage
40	C	Draw conclusions about characters
41	B	Use words with multiple meanings*
42	D	Identify and use antonyms
43	A	Identify details that support a conclusion
44	C	Locate facts and details in a passage
45	B	Draw conclusions about characters
46	D	Locate facts and details in a passage
47	B	Make inferences based on information in a passage
48	C	Identify different types of texts
49	C	Identify and use antonyms
50	A	Use context to determine the meaning of words
51	A	Identify how a passage is organized*
52	C	Understand and analyze word use
53	B	Locate facts and details in a passage
54	A	Identify the author's main purpose
55	D	Identify the purpose of specific information
56	B	Identify different types of texts
57	B	Summarize information given in a passage
58	B	Distinguish between important and unimportant information

*Key Reading Skills

Q1: Prefixes and Suffixes

A prefix is a word part that is placed at the start of a word, such as *un-* or *dis-*. A suffix is a word part that is placed at the end of a word, such as *-less* or *-ly*.

Q3: Main Idea

One way that identifying the main idea is tested is by asking what would be another good title for the passage. The correct answer is a title that describes what the passage is mainly about.

Q11: Simile

A simile compares two things using the words "like" or "as." The phrase "as light as summer's breeze" is an example of a simile.

Q13: Alliteration

Alliteration is a literary technique where consonant sounds are repeated in neighboring words. The phrase "wet and warm" uses alliteration because of the repeated "w" sound.

Q14: Multiple Meanings

Some words have more than one meaning. These words are known as homonyms. All the answer choices are possible meanings for the word *finest*. The correct answer is the one that states the meaning of the word *finest* as it is used in the sentence.

Q16: Fact and Opinion

A fact is a statement that can be proven to be correct. An opinion is a statement that cannot be proven to be correct. An opinion is what somebody thinks about something. The sentence given in answer choice C is an opinion. It describes what the author thinks and cannot be proven to be true.

Q17: Patterns of Organization

There are several common ways that passages are organized. Students will often be asked to identify how a passage, or a paragraph within a passage, is organized. The common patterns of organization are:

- Cause and effect – a cause of something is described and then its effect is described
- Chronological order, or sequence of events – events are described in the order that they occurred
- Compare and contrast – two or more people, events, places, or objects are compared or contrasted
- Problem and solution – a problem is described and then a solution to the problem is given
- Main idea/supporting details – a main idea is stated and then details are given to support the main idea
- Question and answer – a question is asked and then answered

Q20: Identifying Genres (Biography)

A biography is a story of someone's life written by someone other than the person described. This is different to an autobiography, which is the story of someone's life written by that person.

Q28: Multiple Meanings

Some words have more than one meaning. These words are known as homonyms. All the answer choices are possible meanings for the word *fit*. The correct answer is the one that states the meaning of the word *fit* as it is used in the sentence.

Q31: Tone

The tone of a passage refers to the author's attitude. It is how the author feels about the content of the passage. For example, the tone could be playful, sad, cheerful, or witty. In this case, the tone is serious.

Q38: Point of View

This question is asking about the point of view of the passage. There are three main points of view. They are:

- First person – the story is told by a narrator who is a character in the story. The use of the words *I*, *my*, or *we* indicate a first person point of view. *Example: I went for a hike in the mountains. After a while, my legs began to ache.*
- Second person – the story is told by referring to the reader as "you." *Example: You are hiking in the mountains. After a while, your legs begin to ache.*
- Third person – the story is told by a person outside the story. *Example: Jacky went for a hike in the mountains. After a while, her legs began to ache.*

The story has a third person point of view. It is told by someone who is not in the story.

Q41: Multiple Meanings

Some words have more than one meaning. These words are known as homonyms. All the answer choices are possible meanings for the word *positive*. The correct answer is the one that states the meaning of the word *positive* as it is used in the sentence.

Q51: Patterns of Organization

There are several common ways that passages are organized. Students will often be asked to identify how a passage, or a paragraph within a passage, is organized. The common patterns of organization are:

- Cause and effect – a cause of something is described and then its effect is described
- Chronological order, or sequence of events – events are described in the order that they occurred
- Compare and contrast – two or more people, events, places, or objects are compared or contrasted
- Problem and solution – a problem is described and then a solution to the problem is given
- Main idea/supporting details – a main idea is stated and then details are given to support the main idea
- Question and answer – a question is asked and then answered

MULTIPLE CHOICE ANSWER SHEET

EOG Reading Comprehension Practice Test

1	Ⓐ Ⓑ Ⓒ Ⓓ	21	Ⓐ Ⓑ Ⓒ Ⓓ	41	Ⓐ Ⓑ Ⓒ Ⓓ
2	Ⓐ Ⓑ Ⓒ Ⓓ	22	Ⓐ Ⓑ Ⓒ Ⓓ	42	Ⓐ Ⓑ Ⓒ Ⓓ
3	Ⓐ Ⓑ Ⓒ Ⓓ	23	Ⓐ Ⓑ Ⓒ Ⓓ	43	Ⓐ Ⓑ Ⓒ Ⓓ
4	Ⓐ Ⓑ Ⓒ Ⓓ	24	Ⓐ Ⓑ Ⓒ Ⓓ	44	Ⓐ Ⓑ Ⓒ Ⓓ
5	Ⓐ Ⓑ Ⓒ Ⓓ	25	Ⓐ Ⓑ Ⓒ Ⓓ	45	Ⓐ Ⓑ Ⓒ Ⓓ
6	Ⓐ Ⓑ Ⓒ Ⓓ	26	Ⓐ Ⓑ Ⓒ Ⓓ	46	Ⓐ Ⓑ Ⓒ Ⓓ
7	Ⓐ Ⓑ Ⓒ Ⓓ	27	Ⓐ Ⓑ Ⓒ Ⓓ	47	Ⓐ Ⓑ Ⓒ Ⓓ
8	Ⓐ Ⓑ Ⓒ Ⓓ	28	Ⓐ Ⓑ Ⓒ Ⓓ	48	Ⓐ Ⓑ Ⓒ Ⓓ
9	Ⓐ Ⓑ Ⓒ Ⓓ	29	Ⓐ Ⓑ Ⓒ Ⓓ	49	Ⓐ Ⓑ Ⓒ Ⓓ
10	Ⓐ Ⓑ Ⓒ Ⓓ	30	Ⓐ Ⓑ Ⓒ Ⓓ	50	Ⓐ Ⓑ Ⓒ Ⓓ
11	Ⓐ Ⓑ Ⓒ Ⓓ	31	Ⓐ Ⓑ Ⓒ Ⓓ	51	Ⓐ Ⓑ Ⓒ Ⓓ
12	Ⓐ Ⓑ Ⓒ Ⓓ	32	Ⓐ Ⓑ Ⓒ Ⓓ	52	Ⓐ Ⓑ Ⓒ Ⓓ
13	Ⓐ Ⓑ Ⓒ Ⓓ	33	Ⓐ Ⓑ Ⓒ Ⓓ	53	Ⓐ Ⓑ Ⓒ Ⓓ
14	Ⓐ Ⓑ Ⓒ Ⓓ	34	Ⓐ Ⓑ Ⓒ Ⓓ	54	Ⓐ Ⓑ Ⓒ Ⓓ
15	Ⓐ Ⓑ Ⓒ Ⓓ	35	Ⓐ Ⓑ Ⓒ Ⓓ	55	Ⓐ Ⓑ Ⓒ Ⓓ
16	Ⓐ Ⓑ Ⓒ Ⓓ	36	Ⓐ Ⓑ Ⓒ Ⓓ	56	Ⓐ Ⓑ Ⓒ Ⓓ
17	Ⓐ Ⓑ Ⓒ Ⓓ	37	Ⓐ Ⓑ Ⓒ Ⓓ	57	Ⓐ Ⓑ Ⓒ Ⓓ
18	Ⓐ Ⓑ Ⓒ Ⓓ	38	Ⓐ Ⓑ Ⓒ Ⓓ	58	Ⓐ Ⓑ Ⓒ Ⓓ
19	Ⓐ Ⓑ Ⓒ Ⓓ	39	Ⓐ Ⓑ Ⓒ Ⓓ		
20	Ⓐ Ⓑ Ⓒ Ⓓ	40	Ⓐ Ⓑ Ⓒ Ⓓ		

North Carolina Test Prep Reading Workbook

For additional reading test prep, get the North Carolina Test Prep Reading Workbook. It contains 40 reading mini-tests covering all the reading skills on the North Carolina EOG test. It is the perfect tool for ongoing test prep practice and for reading skills revision.

CPSIA information can be obtained at www.ICGtesting.com
Printed in the USA
LVOW09s1525190515

439065LV00003B/66/P